THE EXECUTIVE'S GUIDE
to
Fighting Like a Girl

or

how to claw your way to the top without breaking
a fingernail

I0473910

By: Donald Rump, PhD

Illustrated by Nicole Lee

ISBN-13: 978-1478376279
ISBN-10: 1478376279

DEDICATION

This book is dedicated to St. Marta of the Mainline who stands as a shining example of at least nine of the ten principles.

PREFACE

This may come as a total surprise that despite what some would have you believe, girls fight differently than boys fight. Young boys tend to settle disagreements by simply walking up and thumping the offending party. In today's world this is usually followed immediately by rounds of scolding by their female teachers telling them that "nice" boys don't fight. What the teachers really mean to say is that "nice" boys should not be physically violent, but should fight like girls.

As males mature, they are forced to abandon their natural inclinations. This externally enforced repression of the natural urge to thump the shit out of some bastard who so richly deserves it is the chief underlying cause of things like football and mass murder.

Girls grow up learning to fight in much more clever ways. Girls learn that destroying an opponent through rumor and gossip is much more effective and much less dangerous than physical confrontation. It can even be enjoyed as a group activity. Why risk direct confrontation when a good rumor can socially destroy your opponent? Boys, of course, tend to be clueless.

Women have manuals in how to manipulate men. If you doubt that statement, I invite you to take a close look at any magazine stand in America. Woman's magazines proudly headline "Ten Ways to tell if he likes you" and "five guaranteed ways to drive your man crazy." Men's magazines are almost totally focused on chasing some kind of ball or the latest car. This puts boys at an immense disadvantage in a business world filled with women.

With the increasing number of women in the workforce, it has become vital for an aspiring male executive to understand how to fight like a girl. This short guide will teach you how to defend yourself from the attacks of your female co-workers and give you the tools to destroy your unsuspecting competitors. Pay attention and by the end of the book you will have everything you need to claw your way to the top without breaking a fingernail.

Donald Rump, PhD

CONTENTS

Lesson #1

Always look out for #1

Boys tend to think of the welfare of their gang, team or company. They tend to think of how they can help the team achieve its goals. This is totally wrong. Your personal welfare is much more important. Your goal must not be organizational welfare, but personal advancement. Helping the organization is only important when it helps you advance.

For example, if you are convinced the boss is doing something wrong, don't argue with them. By all means, help them make the mistake. You can later claim that you were only being a good team member and it was your boss who caused the disaster. If things work out, he will get fired and you will get his position. If your boss is not already doing something wrong, help them by finding something.

Always look out for #1

Lesson #2

Always smile sweetly

The key to any good attack is surprise. You cannot position yourself for advancement if others know what you are really thinking. No matter what you are really thinking, agree and keep smiling.

Appearing positive allows two great advantages: #1 it allows you to support any self destructive idea your boss comes up with, (Oh, you want to jump off a bridge. Well, gee everyone will think you're really smart. You will surely get a promotion!)   #2 it allows you to develop the all so important "friend" relationship where you can "share" secrets with your boss.

Always smile sweetly

Lesson #3
Don't be limited to facts

Remember reality is not about facts, it is about other people's perceptions. Facts are not as important as how you "feel" about something.

If your boss refocuses your efforts in a new way and it makes you "sad," then you are perfectly justified in telling everyone in the office your boss watches porn on his computer. It does not matter if you never caught him doing it. You are fully justified in creating your own facts because of the way you were treated. (Note: It is very important to comply with Lesson #2 while creating your own facts.)

Don't be limited to facts

Lesson #4

Make everyone your best friend

Special friends share their deepest thoughts and feelings with each other. They look out for and help each other. That is of course nonsense, but useful.

You want to have each of your co-workers think that they have a special relationship with you. Encouraging them to share their secrets with you.

There are two reasons you want to have all your co-workers share their secrets; #1 so you can use them as allies later and #2 so you can be fully informed as to what others are saying in the office. Remember Lesson #3. You are not limited by facts. Make everyone in the office your special best friend. They should all think they are. None of them should be, Lesson #1.

Make everyone your best friend

Lesson #5

Everyone is disposable

Remember, everyone around you at work is only important in the way they affect your life. If someone within the structure is blocking your progress, feel free to initiate any action you believe required to remove them. Simply because they have a wife, three children, a cat, a dog and a mortgage should not cause you to hesitate one instant in orchestrating their destruction. (They don't really have to be in your way, simply feeling they are an obstacle is sufficient reason to destroy them.)

Everyone is disposable

Lesson #6

Make sure you are at the center

Knowledge is power. As soon as possible become a hub of information flow.

Example, tell one coworker that another co-worker is spreading rumors about them and you will be able to enjoy watching the fight which ensues. By keeping your co-workers fighting each other, and lamenting the discord to your boss, you appear to be the reasonably stable one. It disrupts your office and helps cement your "special best friend" relationship with your boss.

Once you are "special best friend" with your boss, you must share that your most competent co-worker is plotting to replace him/her, thus helping to eliminate your competition.

Make sure you are at the center

12↓ ABU 60.24↓ NKP 3.15T

Lesson #7
Claim responsibility for any success.

No matter what goes right in your organization, you were ultimately responsible for the success. You need to inform everyone that the only reason that achievement was accomplished was because of your contribution. (OK, he might have thought the project up and did all the work, but he would not have succeeded, if I had not filled the coffee pot!) Explain to everyone you are really the reason for the success.

If there is a photo taken, you must make sure you are in the picture. It does not matter if you had anything to do with the project, you can use the photo later as proof you were the key contributor.

Claim responsibility for any success.

Lesson #8

Never admit responsibility for any failure

No matter what goes wrong, never ever admit responsibility. (Yes, the building caught fire and burnt down while I was on duty, but it was not my fault. My boss made me so sad that I had to play with those matches.) Remember, you are not burdened with the truth. No matter how outrageous, simply keep repeating it is not your fault.

Never admit responsibility for any failure

Lesson #9

Never ever go into sales

Sales are vital to every organization and are clearly measured. You do not want to be in sales because it is hard to shift responsibility for failure to someone else (Lesson # 8), and it is very difficult to claim credit for someone else's success (Lesson #7).

If you are absolutely forced into such a position, you need to make sure it is in a managerial position and you have several people below you. You can then take credit for their ideas, if they work, and you can blame them for any failures.

Remember, you can only use one excuse per individual fired. Using the same excuse to fire several individuals will grow old and lose credibility by the third or fourth time.

Never ever go into sales

Lesson #10

"Sleep" with your boss

From the dawn of time, women have found that sleeping with the boss is a wonderful technique, which can make them a super-star literally overnight. (In Madame de Pompadour's case, it seems to have been the night of 25 to 26 February 1745.)

Today, it is even better than before. If a woman sleeps with her boss and does not get what she wants, she simply screams "sexual harassment" and hordes of lawyers appear waiving their business cards.

"Sleep" with your boss

A word of caution: having sex with the boss may be an old and effective female technique, however, unless you are in the entertainment business where it is a requirement, sleeping with another man for organizational advancement is still not viewed totally favorably in some quarters. (This of course does not apply to Democratic politics where performing fellacio is not considered having sex and gay males are protected with more enthusiasm than American Bald Eagles.) By effectively utilizing Lessons 1 through 9 you should not have to "dip the pen in company ink," or worse, allow someone else to "dip his pen in your ink."

There you have it; the ten secrets of clawing your way to the top without breaking a fingernail. You may be passing out literature organizing your local community today, but follow these rules and tomorrow you could be President of the United States! Good Luck!

ABOUT THE AUTHOR

The author holds a PhD in Organization and Management from a prestigious world recognized university; however his name is withheld to protect him from the hoards of screaming, offended harpies who undoubtedly will object to having their secrets revealed.

NOTES

NOTES